Contents

Catch and kill!

Animals are **engineered** by nature to survive in their **habitats**. Some have **adaptations** (features), that make them deadly **predators**. Predators are animals that catch and kill other animals for food.

Predators are found on land, in water and in the sky. Some land predators have strong legs and sharp teeth. These help them to chase down and kill **prey**. Predators in the air are adapted to attack from above. Predators in the water may sting, bite or even give victims an **electric shock**!

ENGINEERED BY NATURE

Deadly Predators

Louise Spilsbury

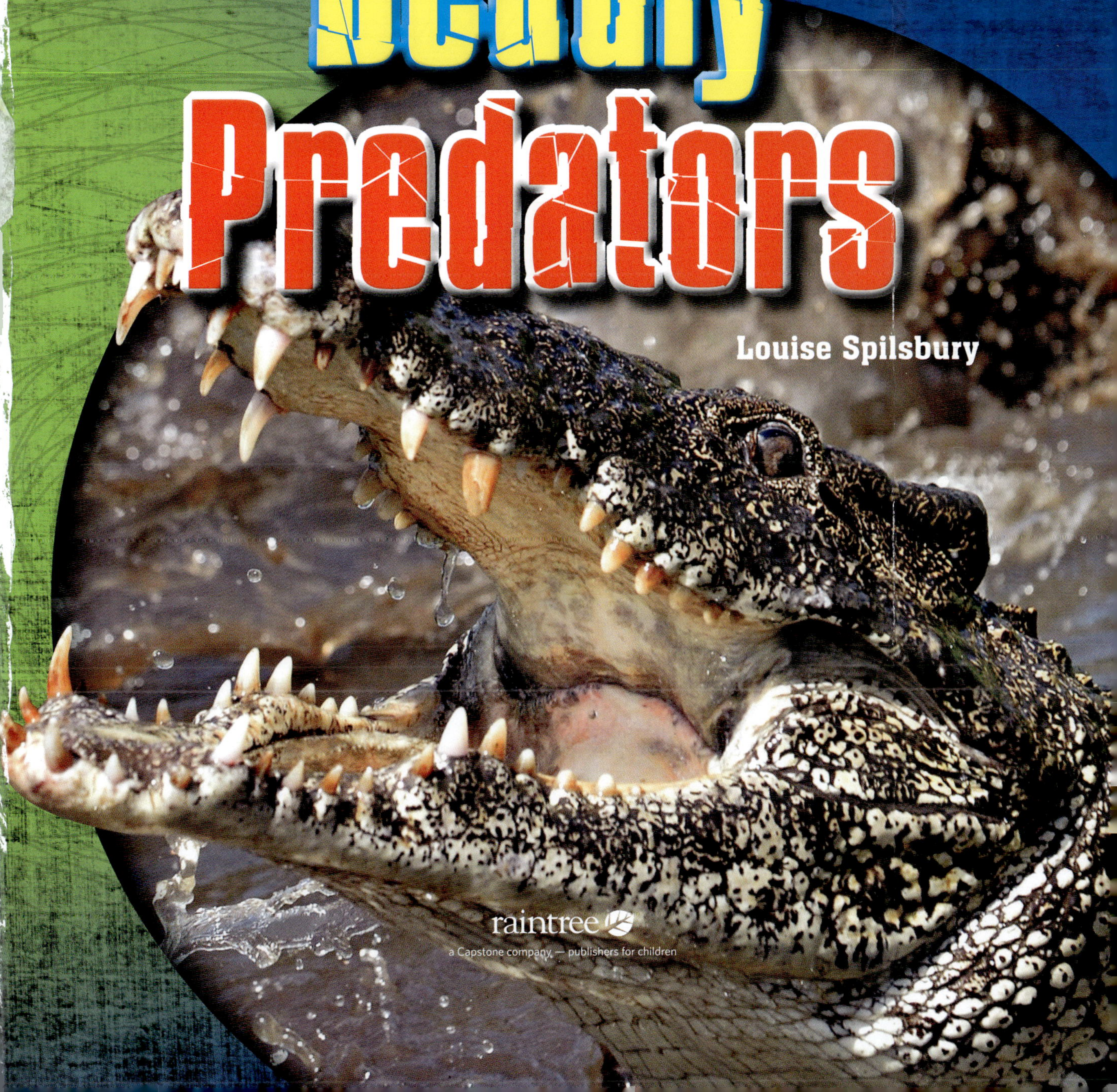

raintree

a Capstone company — publishers for children

Raintree is an imprint of Capstone Global Library Limited, a company incorporated in England and Wales having its registered office at 264 Banbury Road, Oxford, OX2 7DY – Registered company number: 6695582

www.raintree.co.uk
myorders@raintree.co.uk

Produced for Raintree by Calcium
Printed and bound in India

978 1 4747 0049 4 (hardback)
978 1 4747 0061 6 (paperback)

British Library Cataloguing in Publication Data
A full catalogue record for this book is available from the British Library.

Acknowledgements
We would like to thank the following for permission to reproduce photographs: Sergey Uryadnikov/ Shutterstock, front cover, pp. 1, 8–9, 14–15; Alta Oosthuizen/ Shutterstock, pp. 4–5; James Gerholdt/ Getty Images, pp. 6–7; Prosicky/ Shutterstock, p. 9 (middle); Stuart G Porter/ Shutterstock, pp. 10–11; CraigBurrows/ Shutterstock, pp. 12–13; Enrique Ramos/ Shutterstock, p. 15 (bottom); WorldFoto/ Alamy Stock Photo, pp. 16–17; Martin Prochazkacz/ Shutterstock, pp. 18–19; WaterFrame/ Alamy Stock Photo, pp. 20–21; Nick Garbutt/ Nature Picture Library / Alamy Stock Photo, pp. 22–23; MarcusVDT/ Shutterstock, p. 23 (top), Mlorenz/ Shutterstock, pp. 24–25; Michael Lynch/ Shutterstock, pp. 26–27; Olga Visavi/ Shutterstock, pp. 28–29.

Every effort has been made to contact copyright holders of material reproduced in this book. Any omissions will be rectified in subsequent printings if notice is given to the publisher.

FAST FACT

A lion attacks a water buffalo from behind so it does not get stabbed by its prey's sharp horns!

DID YOU KNOW?

A lion's powerful jaws trap prey and deliver a deadly bite. These fierce predators can catch and kill animals much bigger than themselves.

Boa constrictor

A boa constrictor lies in wait at night. It keeps very still. It can smell prey when it is near. It can also sense the body heat that animals give off.

When an animal passes by, the boa strikes. The snake's mouth is lined with sharp teeth that curve backwards. They tightly grasp and hold the prey.

DID YOU KNOW?

A boa grips its victim so tightly that blood and oxygen cannot reach its organs. The victim can die within seconds.

FAST FACT

A boa does not hunt every day. Its body takes four to six days to break down food.

The boa winds its long body around its prey. It slowly squeezes the animal to death. With its mouth wide open, it starts to swallow its victim whole!

Polar bear

A polar bear can smell a bearded seal from around a kilometre away. When it spots the seal, it starts to crawl towards its prey.

If the seal looks around, the polar bear freezes! It keeps very still. The seal cannot see it. The bear's white colouring provides camouflage against the snow and ice.

FAST FACT

A polar bear's claws are curved to catch and trap prey. They also help the bear to grip the slippery ice.

DID YOU KNOW?

A polar bear can smell seals hiding in a den 1 metre (3 feet) under the snow. It uses its massive body to crash through the den's roof. Then it snatches and devours the seals inside!

When the bear is close, it charges! It runs and grabs the seal in its claws or teeth. There is no escape!

Cheetah

A cheetah **stalks** a young gazelle across the grassland. It moves slowly through the tall grass. It silently sneaks up close to its prey.

DID YOU KNOW?

A cheetah is the fastest land animal in the world. It can run 100 metres (328 feet) in just 5.95 seconds.

Suddenly, the cheetah sprints towards the gazelle. The gazelle runs fast, too. The cheetah's powerful legs take huge strides. Its long tail helps it balance when it changes direction at high speed.

The cheetah makes a final dash. Its sharp teeth sink into the gazelle's neck. The chase is over.

FAST FACT

A cheetah's paws have claws that dig into the ground. Their paws also have grooves that grip the ground.

ACTIVITY

Engineering in Practice

The cheetah's paws are designed to grip. This helps it to run fast. Are your shoes engineered to grip, too?

- Find some shoes with different soles. Choose some that are smooth, shiny, rough, grooved and spiked or studded like football boots.
- Take the shoes outside. Rub each sole one way over a dirt or gravel path.
- What do you notice? Which sole grips best? Why do you think that is?

King cobra

The deadly king cobra mainly feeds on other snakes. It hides, and lies patiently in wait for a victim. When it is ready to strike, the snake raises its head.

Suddenly, the cobra darts down. It sinks its sharp, hollow **fangs** into its victim. Like needles, these teeth inject deadly **venom** into the prey.

FAST FACT

A king cobra flicks out its tongue to pick up the scent of its prey.

DID YOU KNOW?

King cobra venom can kill an animal within 30 minutes. One bite contains enough poison to kill 20 people!

The venom in the cobra's bite **paralyses** and kills the victim. Then the snake opens its jaws wide and swallows its food whole.

Crocodile

FAST FACT

A crocodile has more than 60 razor-sharp teeth.

A crocodile does not normally chase prey. It hides in the water and waits. Its eyes, ears and nose are on the top of its head. If its body is under water, it can still see, hear and breathe.

When an animal comes to drink, the crocodile strikes! It uses its tail and strong back legs to spring quickly out of the water. It seizes its victim in its powerful mouth. Its jaws can snap bones like twigs!

DID YOU KNOW?

A crocodile does not use its teeth to chew. Instead, it swallows small stones that help grind up food in its stomach.

Box jellyfish

The box jellyfish swims along. Long **tentacles** hang from its body. These tentacles can be 3 metres (10 feet) long. Each tentacle is covered in about 5,000 tiny darts. Each dart is loaded with powerful venom.

When the tentacles brush against a fish or shrimp, they release a dart. The painful venom **stuns** prey. This stops it from damaging the jellyfish's delicate tentacles. The jellyfish moves its prey towards its mouth, then feasts.

FAST FACT

A box jellyfish is almost invisible in the water because it is pale blue.

DID YOU KNOW?

To move, a jellyfish opens its body and fills it with water. Then it squeezes its body tight, pushing out the water. The jet of water moves the jellyfish forward.

ACTIVITY

Engineering in Practice

Try this activity to see how a jellyfish moves!

- Blow up a balloon, then pinch the end closed so no air escapes.
- Now, let it go!
- The balloon should move quickly forwards, as the air is pushed out of it. This is similar to the way a jellyfish uses jets of water to move.

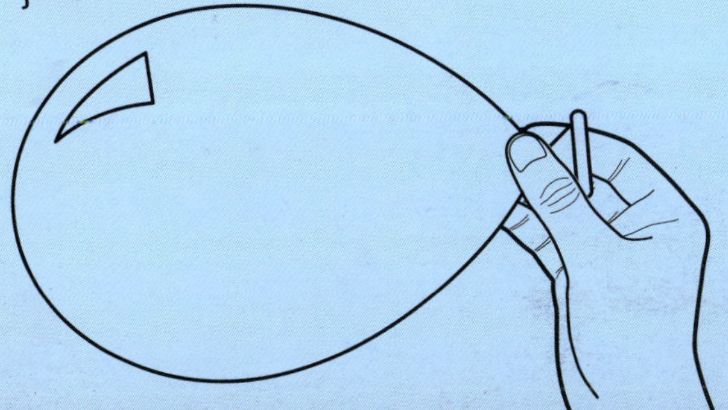

Great white shark

A great white shark swims slowly in the ocean. When it spots a sea lion, it quickly shoots up through the water!

The shark's body is **streamlined**. It is long and thin. This helps it to move through the water like an arrow. As it leaps from the water, the shark opens its mouth.

FAST FACT

A great white shark has about 300 teeth. If it loses a tooth, another one is ready to replace it.

It grabs its prey tightly in several rows of sharp, jagged teeth. Then it crushes, chomps and swallows its victim under water.

DID YOU KNOW?

Great white sharks have an excellent sense of smell. They can smell small amounts of blood from more than 5 kilometres (3 miles) away.

Electric eel

The electric eel lives in muddy pools and rivers. It has poor eyesight. To hunt, it sends out a small **electrical** signal. It uses this like **radar** to find prey.

The electric eel has parts inside its body that store electrical power. It is as though the eel has its own batteries! When a fish comes near, it releases a burst of electricity. This stuns the fish.

Then the electric eel sucks its prey into its mouth, and straight into its stomach!

DID YOU KNOW?

Some electric eels are huge. They can grow to more than 2.5 metres (8 feet) long.

FAST FACT

An electric eel's shock is so powerful it can knock a horse off its feet!

Harpy eagle

A harpy eagle waits in a high rainforest tree. It sits there for hours. When it spots a monkey, it takes flight.

The eagle quickly swoops in for the kill. When it is close to its prey, it stretches out its huge **talons**. It grasps the monkey in these strong claws.

The eagle carries its victim to a high branch. It uses its powerful feet to crush and kill its prey. Then it uses its sharp, hooked beak to feast.

FAST FACT

A harpy's wings measure 2 metres (6.5 feet) across.

DID YOU KNOW?

The harpy eagle's deadly talons are 13 centimetres (5 inches) long. That's as long as a grizzly bear's claws!

Great horned owl

The great horned owl usually hunts at night. It sits on a branch, listening for prey. It twists its head so it can see all around. When it spots a victim, it silently takes off.

DID YOU KNOW?

Huge eyes help owls to hunt for prey in low light. If a great horned owl was as big as a human, its eyes would be the size of oranges!

FAST FACT

A great horned owl eats its prey whole. It then vomits up bones and other parts its body cannot break down.

Its wide wings have a fringe of feathers. These soft feathers reduce the sound of air rushing through them. Prey cannot hear the owl approaching! It grabs its prey in its wide talons and flies off to feed.

Vampire bat

At night, a vampire bat leaves its cave. While it flies, it sends out sounds. The sounds echo back, signalling to the bat where to find a victim.

The bat lands and crawls onto a sleeping cow. The bat's nose senses hot blood flowing under the cow's skin.

The bat sinks its thin, sharp teeth into its victim. It then laps up the blood with its tongue. The bat's saliva keeps the blood from clotting while it drinks.

FAST FACT

To survive, a vampire bat must hunt every one to two days.

DID YOU KNOW?

A vampire bat feeds for about 30 minutes. It does not usually drain enough blood to harm its victim. But its bite can carry deadly diseases!

ACTIVITY

Engineering in Practice

To see how sound reflects off an object, try making an echo yourself.

- Stand a long distance from a wall.
- Clap loudly.
- Listen for the echo. The distance it travels is twice the distance from you to the wall (because the sound has to travel to the wall and back).

Engineered to survive

Adaptations help animals to survive. On land, a polar bear's white colouring helps it to sneak up on seals. A cheetah's long, strong legs help it to chase fast gazelles.

In water, a box jellyfish's tentacles help it to catch prey. A crocodile's teeth stop large prey from escaping. In the air, the owl's silent flight and an eagle's strong talons help them to catch food. Without these features, these animals could not get the food they need to survive.

FAST FACT

If an octopus loses a tentacle, it grows a new one to replace it!

DID YOU KNOW?

An octopus has eight tentacles covered in suckers. It uses its suckers to grip its prey. The octopus then injects venom into its victim.

Glossary

adaptations features or characteristics that an organism has that help it to survive

camouflage colours or patterns that help an animal blend in with its surroundings

clotting becoming thick and sticky to stop blood from flowing

echo bounce a sound back

electric shock injury caused when electricity passes through an animal's body

electrical producing a form of energy called electricity

engineered designed and built

fangs long, sharp teeth

habitats natural areas in which organisms live

paralyse stop an animal from moving

predators animals that catch and eat other animals

prey animals that are eaten by other animals

radar device that sends out radio waves to find out where an object is

saliva spit

stalks hunts slowly and silently

streamlined having a narrow, smooth shape that moves quickly through air and water

stun confuse an animal's senses, usually by a blow

talons long, sharp claws

tentacles long, flexible arms

venom poison produced by some animals

Find out more

BOOKS

Amazing Predators (Animal Superpowers) John Townsend (Raintree, 2012)

Big Cats (DKfindout!), DK (DK Children, 2019)

Killer Whales: Built for the Hunt (Predator Profiles), Christine Zuchora-Walske (Raintree, 2016)

Polar Bear vs Seal (Predator vs Prey) Mary Meinking Chambers (Raintree, 2012)

WEBSITES

www.bbc.co.uk/bitesize/topics/zvhhvcw/articles/zxg7y4j
Learn more about adaptation.

www.dkfindout.com/uk/animals-and-nature
Find out more about animals and nature.

Index